"When pain and disappointment are near, ... y ... g ...arts seek to understand why. Chris Morphew has responded to the age-old question in his excellent little book *Why Does God Let Bad Things Happen?* This small but powerful volume certainly would have helped me when I broke my neck at an early age—I was desperate to make sense of it all as I searched the Bible for answers. Thankfully, Morphew's book addresses the tough topic about God's goodness in a world of great suffering, and he does it in a winsome, easy-to-read way. Yes, it's for young people, but I'm recommending it to people of all ages—and I commend this remarkable book to you!"

JONI EARECKSON TADA, Joni and Friends International Disability Center

"Suffering, sickness, betrayal, racism, war—all make us ask, 'Why is our world so broken?' Chris Morphew gives us gospel responses—not just to answer the questions in our heads but to address the issues in our hearts."

BARBARA REAOCH, Former Director, Children's Division, Bible Study Fellowship; Author, *A Jesus Christmas*

"Chris Morphew is like Tim Keller for teens. In this short book, he tackles some of today's tough questions with Scripture, wisdom and clarity—and just the right amount of fun to keep young readers turning the page. I cannot wait to put this book into the hands of my three children."

CHAMP THORNTON, Pastor; Author, *The Radical Book for Kids* and *Why Do We Say Good Night?*

"Chris is the teacher you wish you had. He gets where you're coming from and takes your questions—and you—seriously. If this is your question, or if you just want to know more about God and the meaning of life, this is the book for you."

DR NATASHA MOORE, Research Fellow, Centre for Public Christianity

"What an excellent series—seriously excellent! I am certain Chris Morphew's chatty style, clear explanations, relevant illustrations and personal insights will engage, inform and equip tweens as they work through some of the big questions they and their peers will be asking."

TAMAR POLLARD, Director for Families, Children and Youth Ministry, Grace Community Church, Bedford

"Bad things happen all around us every day. Perhaps bad things are happening to you or someone you love right now, and you're asking why a good God who is in control of all things doesn't just stop all the badness. Well, I think you've found your next book to read right here. Reading a Chris Morphew book is like sitting with a friend with an open Bible between you, asking all the tough questions that are on your heart and getting solid, straight, honest answers that line up with God's word—answers that bring you to the light and hope and truth of Jesus. I love friends like that!"

COLIN BUCHANAN, Singer/Songwriter

Why does GOD let BAD THINGS HAPPEN?

CHRIS MORPHEW

Illustrated by Emma Randall

For Alegra,
who knows Jesus better than I do.
See you on the other side.

Why Does God Let Bad Things Happen?
© Chris Morphew 2021. Reprinted 2021, 2022.

Published by:
The Good Book Company

thegoodbook.com | thegoodbook.co.uk
thegoodbook.com.au | thegoodbook.co.nz | thegoodbook.co.in

ISBN: 9781784986124 | Printed in the UK

Illustrated by Emma Randall | Design by André Parker

Contents

Chapter 1

? How <u>COULD</u> A ? GOOD GOD ? ALLOW SO MUCH suffering?

Right now, at this very moment, all around the world, things are going wrong.

Bad news is everywhere, and it comes in all shapes and sizes.

Some problems are pretty easy to solve. The littlest kids at the school where I work come to me with heaps of problems—but to be honest, most of them aren't that big a deal. I can usually fix them with a band-aid or sticking plaster, or by telling them to go get a drink of water or to pick someone different to play with.

But as we get older, our problems often get more complicated. If you came to me for advice about a crisis you were having with a friend, and my solution was "Go get a drink of water", I'm guessing you wouldn't come back to me for advice any time soon.

Real life is too complicated for easy answers.

"Chris, can I tell you something?"

The girl's eyes flashed around the room at the other kids, to make sure they wouldn't overhear, and she sighed like her heart was breaking. "I don't think my mum and dad are ever going to love each other again."

She looked miserable, obviously. But more than that, she looked *exhausted*—like all that sadness had worn her out.

A few weeks later, it was official. Her dad had packed up and moved out.

When I asked how she was feeling about it all, she stared at the ground for a long time.

"At least I won't have to listen to them yell at each other anymore."

∿∿∿∿∿∿

I first met Alegra when she was five years old, on her very first day of school.

Alegra was this fun, thoughtful, big-hearted kid—the kind of person who was always way more interested in paying attention to other people than trying to make them pay attention to her. And even though, as one of her teachers, I'd been told that Alegra was recovering from brain surgery and still had a bunch of medical stuff going on, you never would have guessed it by how enthusiastic she always was about school.

But then one day, Alegra didn't come back to school. And as the days went on, we got the news that she *wouldn't* be coming back to school.

Alegra's cancer was back, and this time it wasn't going away.

Not long after her sixth birthday, I found myself standing in a crowded church, surrounded by the hundreds of other friends and family who had gathered for Alegra's funeral.

As we prayed and hugged and cried and said goodbye, the same questions burned through my mind over and over again.

God, how could you let this happen?

Don't you care?

If you've picked up this book, maybe that's your question too.

Maybe you're going through something awful and heartbreaking yourself—or maybe someone you love is. Or maybe it's just that the constant stream of horrible stuff on the news is making you feel anxious and scared about the world, and you don't know how to make sense of it all.

Maybe you wonder where God is in the middle of all this.

When you think about it, all this hurt and brokenness in the world seems like a pretty big problem for God. Or at least, it seems like a pretty big problem for *us*, if we want to believe what God says about himself in the Bible: in particular, that he is all-loving and all-powerful.

Because if God truly is all-loving, then surely he'd want to stop all the suffering that's going on in the world, right?

And if he truly is all-powerful, then he could stop all that suffering whenever he wanted to.

But he hasn't. The world is still full of suffering.

So why doesn't God do something?

Is God not actually as strong as he says he is? Does he want to stop our suffering, but he's too weak to do it?

Or, worse, is he not actually as loving as he says he is? Is he powerful enough to stop our suffering but too cruel to do it?

Or is he both? Is God weak *and* cruel?

Or is all this suffering just proof that God's not really there at all?

Like I said, suffering seems like a pretty big problem for God.

∿∿∿∿∿∿

Here's the thing, though: if your biggest question is *How could a loving, powerful God allow so much suffering?* there's actually a really easy answer.

The whole reason why people ask God for help in the first place—and blame him when he doesn't seem to give it to them—is that God is meant to be so much bigger and wiser and more loving and more powerful than we are.

But if that's true—if God really is that much bigger and wiser than us—then couldn't he have all kinds of good and loving reasons for letting our suffering continue, but which are just too big for us to see right now?

Just because *we* can't see a good reason for our suffering, that doesn't mean there isn't one.

If God is big enough to *blame* for our suffering, he must also be big enough to have great reasons for allowing our suffering to continue that we just don't understand yet.

So there you go.

There's your answer to the problem of suffering.

And I actually think it's a great, solid answer. But if you're anything like me, it probably doesn't feel very helpful. Because what I've just given you is a tidy little "head answer". But suffering isn't just a puzzle for our heads. It's a problem for our hearts.

When we're actually going through something awful, I don't think our biggest question is *How could a loving, powerful God allow so much suffering?*

When it feels like life is falling apart, the cry of our hearts is something bigger and deeper and way more personal: *God, how could you let this happen? Don't you care?*

If we're going to believe that God is as loving and powerful as he says he is, *that's* the question we really need to answer.

And that bigger, deeper, way more personal question is what this book is all about.

Chapter 2

ISN'T suffering JUST a NATURAL PART of LIFE?

To get to the bottom of our questions about suffering, we need to go back to the beginning.

As in, the *very* beginning.

Because before we can make any sense of our suffering, I think we need to ask ourselves another question.

What kind of universe are we living in?

Because here's the thing: if the truth is that we're living in a universe where suffering is just a natural, normal part of life—if things have *always* been like this, if pain and suffering and death are just *how things are*—then we should probably just learn to deal with it.

But what if that's *not* the whole story?

What if there's something bigger going on?

What if we're living in a universe that's broken—a

universe that's *gone wrong* somehow?

When you're going through an awful experience and something deep inside you screams that *things aren't supposed to be like this...* What if you're right?

Because if you *are*—if things *haven't* always been like this—then what if what's been broken in the universe could be fixed again?

In the ancient world, most cultures saw the universe—and the suffering in it—in pretty similar ways. They looked out at the wildness of the world and thought, "The gods must be angry".

Why was the universe so filled with darkness and chaos and fear? Because it was filled with gods and goddesses who made it that way.

The myths and legends of the ancient world were full of angry gods going to war against one another.

One of the oldest and most famous examples is the Enuma Elish, the creation myth of ancient Babylon. There are a few different versions of the story, but basically, if you were a kid living in Babylon three thousand years ago, here's what you were taught about the beginning of the world.

There was this god named Apsu and this goddess named Tiamat, and together they gave birth to a whole bunch of other gods. Pretty soon, though, Apsu started complaining that his kids were too noisy and that they were distracting him from his work, and so he came up with a plan.

He decided to murder them all.

Understandably, Tiamat was a bit upset by this, and so she warned her oldest son, Enki, about Apsu's plan. In response, Enki went off and killed Apsu. He took his dad's dead body and squished it out to make the earth.

When Tiamat heard about Apsu's death, she was furious and decided that killing all her children wasn't such a bad idea after all. She summoned the forces of chaos to create eleven terrible monsters, recruited a god called Kingu to be her army commander and went to war against her kids.

Thankfully for Tiamat's children, a mighty champion named Marduk stepped forward from among them and killed his mum with an arrow (sending two rivers bursting out of her eyes).

Marduk stretched out Tiamat's dead body to make the heavens and then went and killed Kingu too. Out of Kingu's blood, Marduk made the first human beings to be his slaves. Their jobs: to serve the gods and to keep fighting the endless war against the forces of chaos.

And that, the Babylonians said, was how the world was made.

If you lived in Babylon three thousand years ago, understanding all the pain and suffering in the world was *easy*.

"Of *course* the world is scary and chaotic," you'd say. "It's *always* been like this. Look at the gods who made us! What else would you expect?"

At this point you may be thinking, "Well, yeah, but those are just a bunch of old myths! We know that's not where the universe actually came from!"

But there's a pretty popular modern version of this same way of thinking.

Even today, there are still plenty of people who look out at the wildness of the world and figure it must always have been like this.

But these days, people are less likely to blame all the suffering in the world on angry, violent gods, and more likely to say it's because there's no such thing as God at all.

"*Of course* the world is scary and chaotic," they'll say. "It's *always* been like this. We're all just here by accident! What else would you expect?"

Which might help *explain* our suffering.

But it does nothing to help us deal with it.

The writers of the Bible knew the stories that the cultures around them told about gods and goddesses at war. They knew that most people just assumed that the world had always been a place of violence and suffering. But *these writers* viewed the universe completely differently.

The Bible opens with these words:

> *In the beginning God created the heavens and the earth. Now the earth was formless and empty, darkness was over the surface of the deep, and the Spirit of God was hovering over the waters. (Genesis 1 v 1-2)*

Here, instead of multiple gods and goddesses at war, we find one God, living in perfect peace.

We also, apparently, find "the deep" and "the waters".

What's this about? How can there be "waters" if God hasn't even started creating the world yet? Is there some secret ocean out there that was already here before God arrived?

Well, no.

See, in the ancient world, people used water as a symbol for all kinds of darkness and chaos and fear. People saw the ocean as a scary place. It was wild and uncontrollable, and it sank ships and drowned their crews—and so "the deep" and "the waters" became common ways of talking about things that were chaotic and out of control.

And that's exactly what the writer of Genesis is doing here: using water as an image to describe the dark, empty nothingness before the beginning of the universe.

But notice where God is: not *swimming* in the waters and certainly not *drowning* in them. He's not just one more made-up story of a violent, angry god caught up in the chaos of the world.

Instead, on the very first page of the Bible, we find the Spirit of God *hovering over the waters*—soaring peacefully above the darkness and emptiness before creation, preparing to bring it to life.

The Bible continues:

> And God said, "Let there be light," and there was light.
> *(v 3)*

God speaks into the darkness—and whatever God says, that's exactly what happens. And as Genesis goes on—as God takes that emptiness and fills it to the brim with his love and goodness and beauty and creativity—we get our first incredible glimpses of who he is and what he's like.

God is the one who brings light to the darkness. God is the one who brings order to the chaos. God is the one who brings peace to the fear.

The Bible sums up its creation story like this:

> God saw all that he had made, and it was very good.
> *(v 31)*

Whether you were an ancient Babylonian who thought the earth was the body of a murdered god or whether you're someone living in the twenty-first century who doesn't believe in God at all, the Bible paints a life-changing picture of the true beginnings of the world.

We're not here to be slaves, and we're not here by accident.

The universe was created on purpose, out of the overflow of God's love, to be our perfect home. And in the beginning, at least, it was very good.

And so the first thing we need to realise about all the pain and heartbreak in the world is that *it hasn't always been like this*. Sickness and suffering and death *aren't* just natural, normal parts of human life. They're intruders in God's good world.

It was never meant to be this way.

Which brings us to an obvious question: *What went wrong?*

Chapter 3

WHY IS THE WORLD like THIS?

I love superhero stories. I love heroes and villains and epic tales of good triumphing over evil. I love watching the good guys team up to defeat the bad guys. And I love how, in all these stories, there's no villain so terrible that they can't be defeated with enough determination and teamwork, and maybe a cool space laser.

Real life, on the other hand, is way more complicated.

The problem with real life is that the bad guys are usually not big, purple aliens with magic gauntlets or whatever.

In real life, the bad guys tend to look a whole lot more like us.

On the second page of the Bible, after the creation of the universe, the focus zooms in on the first human beings: Adam and Eve.

The first humans weren't made out of blood to be slaves. They were handcrafted by God to be his beloved children. God breathed life into the first people—and that life was a gift that was meant to last forever.

God made people to enjoy lives of perfect friendship with him and with each other: lives where they would join with God, their perfect King, to spend the rest of forever building and growing his very good world.

Which, again, raises the question: *What went wrong?*

If God made the universe to be "very good", then why is our world today so full of pain and suffering?

As we turn to page 3 of the Bible, we find the beginning of an answer:

> *Now the serpent was more crafty than any of the wild animals the LORD God had made. He said to the woman, "Did God really say, 'You must not eat from any tree in the garden'?" (Genesis 3 v 1)*

Actually, that's not what God had said at all, and the serpent knew it.

What God had *really* said was…

> *You are free to eat from any tree in the garden; but you must not eat from the tree of the knowledge of good and evil, for when you eat from it you will certainly die.*
> *(Genesis 2 v 16-17)*

This garden they were talking about was the perfect home that God had created for his first people. The Bible says it was filled with all kinds of trees that were "pleasing to the eye and good for food"—and that it also contained two *other* trees:

> *In the middle of the garden were the tree of life and the tree of the knowledge of good and evil. (Genesis 2 v 9)*

Side by side, in the middle of their new home, God had placed two trees: one tree that would let his people share in his own eternal life, and another tree that he warned them would lead to suffering and death. It was this second tree that he told them not to eat from.

But maybe we need to take a step back here—because all of a sudden, we apparently have magic trees and talking snakes in the story, and this is the point where people often give up reading the Bible and say it's all just a fairytale.

So... is it?

Was the writer of Genesis, the first book of the Bible, actually just like the writers of all those other ancient myths? Is the Bible just another made-up story from an ancient culture who just didn't have enough science to properly understand the world?

Thankfully, the answer is *no*.

There's way more going on here than we've got time to explore right now, but here's the short version: Genesis isn't a science textbook. It's not designed to answer scientific questions about the universe.

It's designed to answer a bunch of way deeper questions about who God is, and who we are, and why the world is how it is.

Genesis is a work of total literary genius, and the answers it gives us are one hundred percent true.

We just need to make sure we're asking the right questions.

∿∿∿∿∿∿

So anyway, back to these two trees in the middle of the garden.

It makes perfect sense that God is offering *life* to his people—but you might wonder what the tree of the knowledge of good and evil is even doing in God's perfect creation.

Why would God put something like that in front of his people?

Well, it turns out that this, too, is part of God's love for them.

See, the problem with eating the fruit on this tree isn't that it's magical or poisonous or cursed or whatever.

The point of these two trees is not the trees at all.

The point of the trees is the choice.

Because real love is *always* a choice, right?

God loves his people with all his heart and soul and mind and strength, but he won't make them love him back—because love that you're forced into isn't actually love at all.

And so God gives Adam and Eve a choice.

They can choose to love God back, to honour him as their true King, to keep trusting that he'll only ever do what's best for them, to keep letting *him* be the one who shows them what's good and evil—and if that's what they choose, then, of course, they'll just keep right on eating from the tree of life.

Or, when a mysterious enemy of God slithers into their home, they can choose to listen to *him* instead of their own Father. They can choose to reject God's loving rule, to reject the life he's holding out to them and to decide what's good and evil for themselves—and they can do *that* by eating from the tree of the knowledge of good and evil.

The point of the trees isn't the trees.

The point of the trees is the choice.

Adam and Eve made their choice:

> *When the woman saw that the fruit of the tree [of the knowledge of good and evil] was good for food*

and pleasing to the eye, and also desirable for gaining wisdom, she took some and ate it. She also gave some to her husband, who was with her, and he ate it.

(Genesis 3 v 6)

The first people choose to ignore and reject God. They choose a life *apart* from God—and God gives them the consequences of their choice. He sends them out of the garden, away from the tree of life (v 22-23), and away from the perfect freedom and happiness that can only be found in him. He says that from now on, their lives won't be "very good" like they were in the beginning—there'll be pain and brokenness mixed in.

Because, remember, human beings were created to rule God's good creation *under him*. They're *central* to God's design for the world. And so the consequences of their separation from God don't just impact them. They impact the whole creation. By cutting themselves off from the source of all life, human beings bring death into the world. By cutting themselves off from the source of all love, human beings bring pain and suffering into the world.

And death and pain and suffering have been here ever since.

At this point, you may be thinking, "Wait. So all of this is *their* fault? Why should we have to live in a world full of suffering just because of *their* stupid choice?"

But the "Adam and Eve" story is not just an explanation of some stuff that happened back in the past.

It also paints a picture of what *all* of us are like.

God gives us all the same choice: to love him like he loves us, and let him be in charge—or to reject God's love and wisdom, and live life our own way.

And in big ways and small, we *all* make the same choice that Adam and Eve did.

We love to divide the world up into "good people" and "bad people". And because we can almost always find someone who seems worse than us, we mostly find it pretty easy to slot ourselves into the "good" category.

But the Bible is way more realistic about us than that.

It's not just that there are a few supervillains *out there* somewhere that God needs to deal with, and then everything will be ok.

Sure, we all act like heroes sometimes. But we all act like villains too.

God is the giver of every good gift. He's the King of the universe, and everything we have comes from him.

But we don't treat God like the King.

Each of us ignores him and forgets him, and makes a mess of any possibility of friendship with him. And God gives us the consequences of our choice. Our messed-up relationship with God leads to messed-up friendships with each other and a messed-up relationship with God's world.

We humans all hurt each other. We all do the wrong thing. We all contribute to what's gone wrong in the world—sometimes by accident and sometimes on purpose.

The line between good and evil cuts straight through the middle of every human heart.

And so where does that leave us?

Well, obviously the world is still a place of incredible beauty—but, just as obviously, it's also a broken mess.

And all that pain and suffering isn't spread out evenly or fairly. Some people are born into poverty while others are born into riches. Some people experience unbearable tragedy while others just face the day-to-day pain and loss and disappointment of living in a broken world.

There's no mapping it out, no escaping it, no cheating the system—because, in the end, no matter *what* we do, death comes for all of us. And in the meantime, you don't automatically earn a better life by being good or a worse one by being bad. Sure, our suffering is sometimes the result of our own bad choices—but just as often it's the result of *other people's* bad choices, and plenty of other times it just seems to come at us at random.

Like I said, it's a mess.

And so the question hanging over Adam and Eve and every human being since is *How will God respond?*

Is our suffering a sign that God has abandoned us—or is there something bigger going on?

And for our clearest glimpse of *that* answer, we need to turn to Jesus.

Chapter 4

WHERE is GOD WHEN WE suffer?

A few years back, I went on a trip to Israel. One of the highlights was taking a boat ride across Lake Galilee. As we approached the far side of the lake, we were hit by a little bit of wind and a tiny sprinkling of rain. It felt like almost nothing—but it was enough to send our boat rocking from side to side.

See, Lake Galilee is the world's lowest freshwater lake— it's over 200 metres below sea level. So when cold winds blow in from the Mediterranean Sea, they rush down between the hills and onto the lake, and whip up *massive* storms on the water.

Thankfully, I managed to avoid getting caught in one of those storms—but 2,000 years earlier, when Jesus and his friends were out on that same lake, it was a different story. A furious, life-threatening storm blew up, and the waves crashed over their boat so that it was nearly swamped.

Some of Jesus' friends were fishermen. They knew how to handle themselves on the water. But apparently, this storm was like nothing they'd never seen before because they were completely terrified.

Jesus, meanwhile, didn't seem too concerned.

> *Jesus was in the stern, sleeping on a cushion. The disciples woke him and said to him, "Teacher, don't you care if we drown?" He got up, rebuked the wind and said to the waves, "Quiet! Be still!" Then the wind died down and it was completely calm. (Mark 4 v 38-39)*

I mean, can you even imagine what that must have been like?

You're moments away from certain death, everything around you is darkness and chaos and fear, and then your friend gets up—and instead of joining you in your panic, he starts *talking to the weather*.

And then the weather does what he says.

Whenever I read this story to one of the younger classes at my school, I always pick a few volunteers to walk over to the window and have a go at changing the weather themselves.

Partly, it's just fun to watch a bunch of five-year-olds yelling at a cloudless sky to please start snowing or whatever, but it also gets the point across.

You cannot change the weather by talking to it. It's impossible. Ridiculous.

Well, unless you're the one who invented the weather in the first place.

By calming this storm on the lake, Jesus gave his friends their most spectacular glimpse yet of his power. They'd already seen him turn water into wine, and heal sick people, and do a whole bunch of other amazing stuff.

They had *not* seen him transform the whole sky just by talking to it. This was a whole new level.

But it was more than that. Jesus wasn't just showing off here. He was making a very particular point about who he was: *You know the God who hovered over the waters before the world was made? The God who spoke, and brought light to the darkness and order to the chaos?*

That same God is still here. He's still with you.

And I'm him.

When the disciples ask if Jesus cares about their suffering, he responds with a spectacular, breathtaking, mind-blowing *yes*.

But he doesn't stop there.

He turns around and asks them a question of his own:

Why are you so afraid? Do you still have no faith?

(v 40)

Which, at first, seems like kind of an odd thing to ask.

Of *course* they were afraid! They'd just almost drowned in an enormous storm!

But when Jesus says, "Do you still have no faith?" what he's asking is *Don't you trust me?*

He's inviting his friends to pull their focus away from the storm for a second and to remember their relationship with him—to remember that they were never just in an enormous storm; they were in an enormous storm *with Jesus*.

Where was God in the middle of all their fear and suffering?

He was right there with them in the boat.

∿∿∿∿∿∿

Remember back at the start of the book, when I gave you that argument to explain how it was totally possible for a loving, powerful God to still allow suffering? Basically, it was that if God is big enough to blame for our suffering, he must also be big enough to have great reasons for allowing our suffering to continue, but which we just don't understand yet.

And remember how I said that, even though that's a pretty solid "head answer", it probably won't help you very much when you're actually suffering?

Well, the good news is that God has given us something way more helpful than a reason or an explanation or an argument. God's truest, best, most helpful answer to all our questions about suffering isn't any of those things.

It's a person. It's God himself, here on earth as Jesus.

Which is way harder than an argument but also way better.

With an argument, all you need to do is understand and agree. The problem is, all the clever arguments and explanations in the world won't actually help very much when your heart is breaking.

A person is different. If you could somehow find a person you could *absolutely trust*; a person you *knew* wouldn't give up on you; a person whose love and care you could *keep* holding on to, even in the middle of the darkest storms in your life; a person with the power to bring you safely through those storms and out other side...

Well, that would change everything.

And that's *exactly* the gift God offers us.

In Jesus, God has given us something infinitely better than an argument or an explanation.

He's given us himself.

In Jesus, we find God *right here with us* in the middle of our pain and suffering, armed with the love and power to put the whole broken mess back together.

Chapter 5

Why doesn't GOD HELP WHEN I ASK HIM TO?

But if Jesus is meant to be God's big answer to the problem of our suffering, then doesn't that just raise a whole bunch of *other* questions?

Like, what does that even *mean*, exactly?

Jesus isn't standing right next to us like he was with his first followers, in a way we can see and hear and touch. We can't just shake him awake when we have a problem.

And, to be honest, there are plenty of times when it seems like *praying* to Jesus doesn't make much difference to our situation either.

If Jesus is God's best answer to our suffering, then what about all the times when it seems like Jesus isn't showing up?

What about all the times when we call out to God for help, and it feels like he's not even listening?

~~~~~~~~~~

One of Jesus' closest friends was a man named John.

John was there on the boat when Jesus calmed the storm—and he was there to see pretty much every other amazing miracle Jesus did too. Later in life, he wrote a biography of Jesus—it's the book of the Bible we call "John".

In his book, John recounts the incredible true story of a man named Lazarus and his two sisters, Mary and Martha.

When Lazarus becomes seriously ill, his sisters send word to Jesus. These guys are friends with Jesus already. They've seen him heal people before, so they know that if anyone can help Lazarus, Jesus can.

Jesus gets their message, and, at first, his response seems like good news:

> When he heard this, Jesus said, "This sickness will not end in death. No, it is for God's glory so that God's Son may be glorified through it." (John 11 v 4)

Great news! Lazarus isn't going to die!

But then things take a bit of a turn:

> Now Jesus loved Martha and her sister and Lazarus. So when he heard that Lazarus was sick, he stayed where he was two more days. (v 5-6)

Hang on. *What?*

Jesus' response to his friends' desperate call for help is to just wait around for two whole days before he does anything about it. It seems cruel, right?

But notice that little word in the middle there: "So".

John doesn't say, *Jesus loved his friends. BUT he stayed where he was.*

John says, *Jesus loved his friends. SO he stayed where he was.*

As in, *because* Jesus loved his friends, he stayed where he was.

Apparently, even the waiting was part of Jesus' loving plan to help his friends.

But how in the world does that make sense?

By the time Jesus gets to Bethany, the hometown of Lazarus and his sisters, it's already too late. Lazarus is dead, and his body has been sealed away in the family tomb.

Imagine the heartbreak in Martha's voice as she comes out to meet Jesus and says out loud the words that everyone else is thinking:

> *Lord ... if you had been here, my brother would not have died. (v 21)*

Don't worry, though. Lazarus is going to be fine.

I know it looks bad, but I've already skipped ahead and read the ending of the story.

Turns out Martha didn't need to be worried or sad after all.

That's the handy thing when you're reading about events that happened 2,000 years ago—if you want to know the ending of a person's story, you can just skip ahead a few paragraphs.

It's like that with the story of the storm. As you see Jesus' friends in the boat shaking him awake and screaming, "Don't you care?" you can say, "Well, yeah, but they didn't need to panic, because Jesus was about to save them".

Here's the thing though: *they didn't know that.*

We might know the ending to the story—the part that makes it all make sense—but they didn't.

In the middle of the storm, they couldn't see the rescue yet.

All they could see was the storm.

And (sorry to spoil the ending for you, but…) as you read about Martha telling Jesus, "Lord, if you had been here, my brother would not have died," you can say, "Well, yeah, but she didn't need to panic, because Jesus was about to solve that one too".

But again, remember, *she didn't know that.*

Martha had a plan for how she thought things should go,

but Jesus had a different plan. She had a timetable for when she thought Jesus should come to help her brother, but Jesus had a different timetable.

And so Martha had to wait.

She had to wait while her brother died.

She had to wait, not knowing the end of the story, because she wasn't there yet. She was still stuck in the middle of it.

∿∿∿∿∿

And this is the problem we face constantly in our own lives too: we're stuck in the middle of them.

We're not at the end of *our* stories yet, which means we can't yet see the full picture of what God's going to do. And what makes this even harder is that Jesus' plans and timetables are so often way different to ours.

We ask for God's help and healing—but then, so often, we just have to *wait* for Jesus to show up and do what he chooses to do, when he chooses to do it.

And there are times when that waiting feels like drowning.

There are times when it feels like death.

There are times when it feels like God could have shown up to help, but he *didn't*—or that by the time he showed up, it was too late to make any difference.

And at that point, we have a choice.

We can choose to accuse God of being weak, or cruel, or of not even being there at all.

Or we can choose to keep putting our trust in Jesus, while we wait to see what he's going to do next. We can choose to keep trusting that Jesus loves us, that he's in control, and that he knows what he's doing even when we have *no idea in the world* what that might be.

We can choose to trust that even the waiting is part of Jesus' loving plan to help his friends.

Martha makes her choice.

> *"Lord," Martha said to Jesus, "if you had been here, my brother would not have died. But I know that even now God will give you whatever you ask." (v 21-22)*

Despite everything, even though it seems like there's no way something so awful and broken could ever be made right, Martha doesn't give up on Jesus.

And then Jesus makes Martha a promise that turns everything upside down: "Your brother will rise again" (v 23).

Martha's story isn't over.

Jesus is going to bring Lazarus back to life.

Chapter 6

DOES GOD ACTUALLY care ABOUT my SUFFERING?

Already in this book, we've seen that God cares deeply about the mess his world is in—and that, in Jesus, he's come to earth to put things right again.

Which, obviously, is great news.

But I think we need to go a level deeper.

Because if you're anything like me, you don't just need to know that Jesus cares about *the world*, or even that he cares about *people* in some kind of general way.

If I'm actually going to trust Jesus in the middle of my suffering, I need to feel sure that he cares about *me*.

Let's go back to the story about Lazarus. At first, when Jesus tells Martha that her brother will rise again, she's not that excited—but that's only because she doesn't understand what he's saying. She tells Jesus, "I know he will rise again in the resurrection at the last day" (John 11 v 24).

Martha remembers God's promises about a great resurrection day at the end of time, when all God's people will be brought back to life again. And so when Jesus talks about Lazarus coming back to life, she assumes that's what he means.

She thinks Jesus is saying one of those things that people say to comfort each other at funerals, like, "He's gone to a better place", or "We'll see him again one day".

And Martha wasn't *wrong* about that resurrection day— but when Jesus said, "Your brother will rise again", he didn't mean then.

He meant *that day*.

> *Jesus said to her, "I am the resurrection and the life. The one who believes in me will live, even though they die." (v 25)*

Jesus told Martha that, yes, there *would* be a future day when the dead come back to life again—but she wouldn't have to wait until then, because that resurrection power was inside of Jesus *right at that moment*.

God's promises about new life after we die are as true and solid and real as Jesus himself—and Jesus was about to give Martha a glimpse of that future reality, right there and then.

∿∿∿∿∿

It would be tempting to just skip ahead and show you the part where Jesus brings Lazarus back to life—but there's something else I want you to see first.

Because you might expect this story to be all excitement and celebration from here on, but that's *not* what we see.

At least, not right away.

Check out what happens when Martha goes to get her sister Mary:

> *When Mary reached the place where Jesus was and saw him, she fell at his feet and said, "Lord, if you had been here, my brother would not have died."*
>
> *When Jesus saw her weeping, and the Jews who had come along with her also weeping, he was deeply moved in spirit and troubled. "Where have you laid him?" he asked.*
>
> *"Come and see, Lord," they replied.*
>
> *Jesus wept. (v 32-35)*

How does John describe Jesus' reaction to the pain and heartbreak of his friends?

Not, *Jesus' eyes welled up a bit.*

Not, *A single sympathetic tear rolled down Jesus' face.*

And absolutely not, *"What are you all so upset about?"*

It says, "Jesus *wept*".

And with these two short words, John gives us a powerful glimpse of God's response to our suffering.

∿∿∿∿∿∿

When you're going through something horrible, what do you imagine God's reaction to be?

Do you picture him ignoring you?

Do you see him standing back with his arms folded, saying, *Well, this is what you get for making such a mess of things*?

Do you imagine him not really getting it? After all, he's the great big invincible God of the universe—how would he know what it's like to suffer?

Or do you see the truth that Jesus shows us about God?

Do you see God with tears in his eyes?

Do you see him *deeply moved* by your suffering?

Do you hear Jesus' promise that it *really can* all be ok in the end—and that, in the meantime, he offers to be right there with you in the middle of all the pain and the mess?

∿∿∿∿∿∿

Jesus friends' assume that he's weeping because he thinks it's all over: that Lazarus's death is the end of the story. They're still focused on their situation instead of on Jesus.

They reach the tomb where Lazarus is buried, a cave with a stone laid across the entrance, and Jesus tells them to roll the stone away. But even now, they don't understand what he's about to do. Martha reminds Jesus that Lazarus has been buried for four days by now—the smell in there is going to be terrible!

But Jesus tells them to trust him.

So they took away the stone. Then Jesus looked up and said, "Father, I thank you that you have heard me. I knew that you always hear me, but I said this for the benefit of the people standing here, that they may believe that you sent me."

When he had said this, Jesus called in a loud voice, "Lazarus, come out!" The dead man came out, his hands and feet wrapped with strips of linen, and a cloth around his face.

Jesus said to them, "Take off the grave clothes and let him go." (v 41-44)

And maybe now we can start to make sense of why Jesus waited those two extra days before he came to help Lazarus—why he let Lazarus die before coming to his rescue.

Jesus had healed plenty of people before—even people who were miles away from him—so obviously Jesus *could* have kept Lazarus from ever dying in the first place. But he didn't. He brought Lazarus *through* death and out the other side.

And even though the whole experience was sad and scary, Jesus used it to teach his friends more about himself—to show them his power and his love, and just how much they could trust him.

And even though Mary, Martha and Lazarus never would have *chosen* their situation, when all was said and done, I bet if you'd asked them, they would have said it was worth it.

Looking back, I bet Mary, Martha and Lazarus could see how even the waiting was part of Jesus' loving plan to help them—because, thanks to the waiting, they didn't just get to see a healing.

They got to see a resurrection.

Here's the thing, though: Jesus might have brought Lazarus back from the dead—but he didn't bring back little Alegra from my kindergarten class when she died of brain cancer.

A few months ago, I got together with Alegra's family and friends to mark her eighth birthday. It was a beautiful morning, all except for one thing: Alegra wasn't there.

The biographies of Jesus are full of these amazing miracle stories where Jesus just says a word, and someone's whole situation gets fixed. But if you're anything like me, you can think of plenty of situations where you *really* could have used a miracle like that, but you didn't get one.

If Jesus *cares* enough to put an end to our suffering (which, as we've seen, he obviously does) and if he's *powerful* enough to put an end to our suffering (which, as we've seen, he obviously is), then why hasn't he done it? Or why doesn't he do it *now*?

Why doesn't Jesus do for us what he did for Lazarus?

∧∧∧∧∧∧

To answer that question, we need to think about movie trailers.

Like I've told you already, I'm a big fan of superhero movies. Whenever a trailer comes out for the latest Marvel movie, I drop whatever I'm doing and watch it.

I love these trailers.

But the trailer is not a replacement for the movie.

When the new movie finally comes out and my friends start making plans to go see it, I don't say, "No thanks. I'll just stay home and watch the trailer again".

Because the trailer is great and everything, but the whole point of a movie trailer is to get you excited about the movie. It's to help you look forward to the bigger, better, way more exciting thing that's still coming in the future.

Jesus' miracles are kind of like that.

I absolutely believe that Jesus can still do miracles today, but the miracles we see Jesus do in the Bible aren't promises that God will do the same thing for us every time we ask—because Jesus' miracles aren't God's ultimate solution to the problem of our suffering. There's a bigger, better, way more exciting thing still coming.

Jesus' miracles aren't the movie. They're just the trailers.

The main event—the thing all those miracles point forward to—is that resurrection day that Martha was talking about: the day in the future when Jesus will return to raise the dead, to wipe out all evil everywhere, and to make this world our perfect, eternal home again.

So if we're wondering why Jesus doesn't step in and put an end to *our* suffering, the answer is that he *will*. Waiting for that day might feel excruciating right now, but like any good movie trailer, Jesus' miracles are promises that this resurrection day really *is* coming—and they also give us a bunch of hints and glimpses of what that day is going to be like.

This is exciting, incredible, life-changing stuff!

But, as one of my students pointed out after class a few months ago, there's just one slight problem...

Chapter 7

HOW CAN GOD GET
✝ RID of suffering
WITHOUT GETTING
RID of US?

It was a Wednesday afternoon, and I'd been having a long and winding conversation with one of my Year 5 classes, talking through a bunch of their questions about God—but now the bell was about to ring, so I said, "Sorry guys, hands down. We'll pick this up again next lesson."

One girl called out, "But I've got a question!"

"I know you do," I said, "but unfortunately, we've run out of—"

"But it's the *most important question!*"

I said, "Everyone's question is important."

And she said, "*Please*, Mr Morphew! *It's a matter of life and death!*"

And I said, "Ask me later."

And so as we were packing up, she came and asked me

her question—and it turns out it kind of *was* the most important question.

She said, "Mr Morphew, you say Jesus is going to come back one day and get rid of all the bad stuff in the world, right?"

And I said, "Yes..."

And she said, "Ok, but aren't we the ones who do most of that bad stuff?"

And I said, "Well, yeah, that's true."

And she said, "Right, but then if Jesus is going to come back and get rid of all the bad stuff in the world... won't that mean he has to get rid of us?"

∿∿∿∿∿

Think of it like this: imagine there's a student at your school who's having an absolutely miserable time, being bullied every single day by some other kids. And imagine that, every day, this student goes to their teacher and tells them what's happening and, every day, the teacher responds in the exact same way.

"Yeah, look, I know those boys hurt you and tease you and steal your stuff... but I'm not one of those mean, strict teachers. I'm a *nice* teacher! So I'm not going to get them into trouble for any of that. I'm just going to let them keep doing it."

What would you say about a teacher like that?

You'd say they were doing a *terrible* job, right?

A good teacher doesn't just turn a blind eye to bullying. A good teacher looks at the wrong things their students do to each other and says, "This has got to stop".

∿∿∿∿∿

The fantastic news for us is that Jesus is nothing like that terrible teacher. Sickness and suffering and death are intruders in God's good world, and the story's not over until they're wiped out, once and for all.

Which is why, when Jesus returns, it will be to judge the world.

The Bible puts it like this:

> *For we must all appear before the judgment seat of Christ, so that each of us may receive what is due us for the things done while in the body, whether good or bad.*
> *(2 Corinthians 5 v 10)*

Now, that word "judgment" makes a lot of people uncomfortable—but when the Bible talks about Jesus judging the world, it's not talking about Jesus standing there with a clipboard and a frown, looking for excuses to punish people for stuff.

It's talking about Jesus being our loving King who looks at the evil in the world and says, "This has got to stop".

If Jesus looked out at all the world's evil and just said, "Yeah... but I'm a kind and loving God! So I'm not going to get them into *trouble* for any of that. I'm just going to let them keep doing it", he wouldn't actually be a kind and loving God at all!

If Jesus is truly the God of love—which he is—then he also needs to be a God who wipes out evil—which he is.

But if Jesus is going to wipe out all evil and suffering, that means he'll need to wipe out all the *causes* of evil and suffering. And since we all contribute to the evil and suffering in the world...

How can Jesus wipe out all evil and suffering without wiping *us* out too?

To save the world, Jesus had to die.

When I say that Jesus came to be with us in our suffering, I don't just mean that he's with us while *we* suffer (although that's absolutely true).

I mean that Jesus suffered too.

Jesus doesn't just understand our suffering from the *outside*. He understands it from the inside because he's been through it too.

Have you been betrayed? So has Jesus. One of his closest friends sold him out to his enemies so they could arrest him.

Have you been sick with sadness and fear? So has Jesus.

As he waited for those enemies to come and drag him away, Jesus became so overwhelmed with sorrow that he couldn't even stand up.

Have you been abandoned? So has Jesus. As soon as his enemies arrested him, his friends (who'd *just* promised they'd never leave him) ran away and pretended they didn't even know him.

Have you been treated unfairly? So has Jesus. Even though he was completely innocent, he was dragged in front of a court who'd already decided he was guilty, and they sentenced him to death.

Have you been emotionally hurt? So has Jesus. As a sick joke, he was dressed up as a king and paraded around while people mocked and spat on him.

Have you been physically hurt? So has Jesus. He was beaten up and whipped. Nails were hammered through his hands and feet, and he was hung up on a cross to die.

When you suffer, it can be easy to feel like God is distant or uncaring—but nothing could be further from the truth.

When you suffer, Jesus *gets* it. He knows what you're going through from the inside out because he's been through it too.

But there's more.

Jesus didn't just come to suffer *with* us.

He came to suffer *for* us.

∿∿∿∿∿

How can Jesus wipe out all evil and suffering without wiping us out too?

Because 2,000 years ago, on a hill outside Jerusalem, all of God's judgment came down—all of the right and fair consequences for the evil we do to each other and the evil we do to him.

But it didn't come down on us.

It all came down on Jesus instead.

On the cross, Jesus—God himself—went through the ultimate suffering for us so that we would never have to face it.

On the cross, we see Jesus, the innocent, being treated as though he were guilty—so that if we put our trust in him, we, the guilty, can be treated as though we're innocent. We don't have to pay for all the ways in which we make a mess of our friendships with God and each other, because Jesus has already paid with his life.

Which means that now, if we put our trust in Jesus, we can *look forward* to the great day when he'll return to wipe out all the bad stuff, because we know that our bad stuff has already been taken care of.

Chapter 8

Will the WORLD be THIS WAY FOREVER?

Two days after Jesus' death, his closest friends were hiding in an upstairs room with the door bolted shut. Their leader was gone, and they were terrified that the people who killed Jesus were going to come for them too.

Suddenly, Jesus appeared among them.

They freaked out, thinking he was a ghost (which, since they'd just watched him die and now he was popping up inside a locked room, was kind of a reasonable reaction, if you ask me). But Jesus calmly proved to them that he was very much alive:

> He said to them, "Why are you troubled, and why do doubts rise in your minds? Look at my hands and my feet. It is I myself! Touch me and see; a ghost does not have flesh and bones, as you see I have."

> When he had said this, he showed them his hands and feet. And while they still did not believe it because of joy

> *and amazement, he asked them, "Do you have anything here to eat?" They gave him a piece of broiled fish, and he took it and ate it in their presence. (Luke 24 v 38-42)*

Jesus had real flesh and real bones. He could eat real food. He hadn't returned to his friends as something *less* than what he was before. He was *all* the way back—a real human being, in a real human body that had been through death and had come out the other side.

And Jesus hadn't just come back to life like Lazarus, who eventually grew old and died again. Jesus had come back to life in a *transformed body* that could never get sick or get hurt or grow old or die again—a body that would last forever.

A body that's still alive today.

And here's the most mind-bending thing of all: thanks to Jesus' resurrection, *you* can be resurrected too.

If you're trusting in him, you too will be brought back to life in a *transformed body* that will never get sick or get hurt or grow old or die again.

"I am the resurrection and the life," Jesus said. "The one who believes in me will live, even though they die" (John 11 v 25).

It can be so easy to believe that suffering and death are permanent, unchangeable realities in our world—that this is just *how things are*. But Jesus insists that things *haven't* always been this way, and they *won't* always be this way.

Jesus has come once to die in our place and make a way for us to come home to God, and he's coming back to put this whole broken mess back together and make the world our perfect home again.

That's the promise of the resurrection.

That's where the *whole universe* is heading.

Which means that *every single bit* of our pain and suffering in this world—no matter how much it might run you down or wear you out or break your heart—*everything* about our lives and our world that's sad and broken and painful and wrong—is also *temporary*.

Yes, our world is broken. Yes, our suffering hurts. Yes, it's awful. Yes, it's wrong. But it does not have the last word, and it *will not last forever*.

Not if you put your trust in Jesus.

But if Jesus is going to return and put the whole world right again, what's to stop human beings from just messing everything up again like they did the first time?

Because when Jesus returns, he's not just going to transform the world on the outside—he's going to transform his people's hearts on the inside.

Think of it this way: if someone came up to you and said, "Hey, do you think we should cut our own arms off for fun?" your answer would obviously be "No".

Why? Because keeping your arms attached to your body is a better way to live—and all the way down to the deepest part of you, you *know* that's true. It's so completely obvious that cutting your arms off is a *terrible* plan that you'd never dream of doing it.

And if we're one of Jesus' followers, then, when he returns, we'll be so transformed by his love that *that's* how we'll feel about turning our backs on God.

Whether it's eating from a tree God told us not to eat from, or lying, or stealing, or talking about our friend behind their back, the whole reason any of us ever reject God and do our own thing is that, deep down, we don't really believe that God loves us as much as he says he does. We don't believe that God knows best, and we want to put ourselves in charge instead.

But when Jesus returns, his people will be so *sure* of God's love for us that ignoring or disobeying him will be as unnatural to us as cutting off our own arms—which means that the day Jesus returns really will be the day our suffering ends, once and for all.

But whenever I talk about this stuff at school, the same question comes up over and over and over again. Maybe it's the question running through your mind too.

Because the thing about Jesus' promises—new life forever in new bodies in a world without sadness or suffering or death—is that, when you think about it, they sound a whole lot like the ending of a fairytale.

And they all lived happily ever after.

Which is really uplifting and beautiful and whatever, but the obvious downside of fairytales is that they *aren't real*.

And so maybe Jesus' promises don't just sound amazing to you. Maybe they sound impossible.

Maybe the *real* question here is, *Isn't this all just a little bit too good to be true?*

~~~~~~~~~

Here's a different way to think about that question: a little while back, my friends Kerryn and Andrew had a baby. They brought little Josiah home from the hospital, and now he's living with his amazing parents, who love him.

But imagine that didn't happen. Imagine there was a terrible mix-up at the hospital, and instead of going home with Kerryn and Andrew, Josiah went home with a horrible family who didn't care for him at all.

Imagine that, instead of giving him food to eat, they only ever fed him dog food. And imagine they kept their kitchen locked so he never even got to see what real food looked like.

And imagine every day, when he complained about eating his dog food, he was told, "This is just what food is".

What would happen?

Well, he'd be unhealthy, and sick, and sad.

But he'd also think, "This is just the way things are".

He might have a sneaking suspicion that there *must* be something better out there, but because all he'd ever known was dog food, he'd just think eating dog food was totally normal.

But now imagine that after a few years, Kerryn and Andrew found Josiah and got him back and brought him home. And imagine, as they were driving him home, they started talking to him about real food—about all the amazing things to eat that were waiting for Josiah when he got back to his true home.

It would sound amazing. But it would also be impossible for Josiah to imagine. He'd probably find himself struggling to believe it.

The whole way home, he'd be asking himself, "Isn't all this too good to be true?"

But then he'd get home.

And he'd see it.

And he'd taste it.

And he'd realise the truth.

The dog food wasn't all there was. It was all he'd ever known, but it wasn't all there was. The truth was that there was a whole world of delicious, life-giving, *real* food out there, just waiting to be discovered.

It can be hard for us to even *imagine* a future as good as the one Jesus promises his followers, let alone believe in it—but that's not because it's too good to be true. It's because a world of sickness and suffering and death is all we've ever known.

In a world full of bad news, bad news is just easier to believe.

But Jesus has entered into real history to show us that a better world isn't just possible—it's already on its way.

We've been lost for a long time—long enough to believe that a world full of suffering is the only world there is. But through the life, death and resurrection of Jesus, God our Father has come to bring us home.

Chapter 9

WHAT DIFFERENCE does ANY of this MAKE TODAY?

Imagine two kids get called into the principal's office, one at a time.

"Listen," the principal tells the first kid, "we've got a problem: the cleaners have gone on strike and we've got no one to clean the school toilets. Well, except we do now, because... congratulations! You've just been recruited for the job! For the rest of the year, you'll be working as a toilet cleaner instead of a student. Here's your scrubber and bucket. Off you go."

The first kid leaves, and the second kid gets called in. The principal tells him the exact same thing she told Kid #1, but at the end she adds, "Oh, and by the way, we realise this is probably kind of a hassle for you, so at the end of the year, we'll give both of you one hundred million dollars."

Now, as those two students get to work scrubbing toilets, how are they going to feel?

Well, obviously Kid #1 is going to be miserable. All this horrible work!

But Kid #2 is going to see things completely differently. He's going to be joyful, even in the middle of his suffering— not because his work is any less horrible but because he knows the horrible work is not the whole story.

Kid #2 knows the ending to his story is going to be so good that it's going to make all this suffering seems like just a distant memory. Seeing that bigger picture doesn't take away Kids #2's suffering, but it has the power to completely transform the way he goes through it.

And the same is true for us.

We're living in a strange, in-between part of history.

Jesus has already come to earth the first time. Through his life, death and resurrection, he's already done everything it takes for us to be welcomed back home into friendship with God—and he's given us all kinds of hints and glimpses about what the world's going to be like when he comes back the second time to make everything right again.

But we're not there yet.

We're still here, in between, waiting for Jesus to come back.

And Jesus was absolutely realistic about what our lives in this in-between time would be like. The night before Jesus was nailed to the cross, he had a long conversation with his friends about what was about to happen to him, and to them—and he wrapped it all up with these words:

I have told you these things, so that in me you may have peace. In this world you will have trouble. But take heart! I have overcome the world. (John 16 v 33)

Jesus doesn't say his followers *might* have trouble. He says they *will*. We should *expect* trouble in our lives because the world is a messed-up place full of messed-up people.

But that's not the whole story—because Jesus has overcome the world.

Jesus has overcome *death itself.*

And right now, today, in the middle of all the world's brokenness, Jesus is still in charge—even when it might not always look that way to us.

As Jesus' friends were shaking him awake in the boat, they couldn't see that Jesus was in control. But that's just because they weren't at the end of their stories yet.

As Mary and Martha watched their brother Lazarus die, they couldn't see that Jesus was in control. But that's just because they weren't at the end of their stories yet.

And as we go through pain and suffering in our own lives—as we wonder how Jesus could possibly be good and kind and in control in the middle of all *this*—we need to remember that we're not at the end of *our* story yet either.

One day, Jesus will return to make the whole world new again:

> *[God] will wipe every tear from [his people's] eyes. There will be no more death or mourning or crying or pain, for the old order of things has passed away.*
> *(Revelation 21 v 4)*

So here and now, today, even when things feel *completely* awful and out of control, we can take heart. We can be brave. We can find peace and even joy—not because our suffering is any less horrible but because we know it's not the whole story.

A writer in the Bible named Paul puts it this way:

> *I consider that our present sufferings are not worth comparing with the glory that will be revealed in us.*
> *(Romans 8 v 18)*

In other words, if you're putting your trust in Jesus, you can know for certain that the ending to your story is going to be *so good* that it's going to make all this suffering seem like just a distant memory—and that, in the meantime, even the waiting is part of Jesus' loving plan for us.

Seeing that bigger picture doesn't take away our suffering, but it has the power to completely transform how we go through it.

In the meantime, God makes us another promise:

> *And we know that in all things God works for the good of those who love him, who have been called according to his purpose. (Romans 8 v 28)*

And as we put our trust in Jesus, God promises to take every single thing that happens to us—the good, the bad, and the absolutely heartbreaking and awful—and weave it all together into the incredible story of love and rescue that he's telling through all of history.

Like I said before, we can't just shake Jesus awake when we have a problem. But we also don't need to. We might not be able to see Jesus face to face yet, but he's still right here with us, day by day, moment by moment, through his Spirit.

And Jesus can use even our worst suffering to help us more clearly understand his love for us, and to help grow his followers up into people who are more and more like him (v 29)—people who are better able to share his love with a hurting world. I've seen this happen over and over again in my own life.

I've seen God take the horrible bullying I experienced at school and use it to shape me into a more caring, empathetic person, who's better able to help *my* students when they're going through hard times.

I've seen God take scary, uncertain situations and use them to help me grow in the peace of trusting that he's always in control.

I've seen God bring me through situations where all my plans got smashed to pieces, and I've discovered on the other side that, all along, God was working on a bigger, better plan than I ever could have seen coming.

This doesn't mean for one second that all things that happen to us *are* good—because, as we've been seeing all along, Jesus hates the world's pain and brokenness even more than we do.

What it means is that God will use all things that happen to us *for* good—that our suffering might be awful, but it doesn't have to be wasted.

And in the words of one of my favourite writers, somehow, when all is said and done, "the world will be even more beautiful for once having been so sad".

The ultimate example of all this is the cross.

When things go wrong—when my life feels like it's falling apart—I find it so easy to think, "It's all over! Everything is ruined!"

But Jesus won't let me get away with that kind of thinking because—well, look at the cross! Look at when the *worst thing ever* happened, and God *himself* was arrested and beaten up and killed.

When it most seemed like it was all over—when it *most* seemed like everything was ruined—God turned it all around and transformed it into the greatest day in history: the defeat of death, once and for all!

And if God can bring something *that good* out of something *that bad*—then who knows what he might be getting ready to do with the pain and suffering in our lives?

Chapter 10

SOMETHING BETTER than a THOUSAND ANSWERS

Almost two years to the day after Alegra passed away, I sat up at the front of a Year 2 classroom, chatting with a bunch of her old classmates.

"I want you to imagine something," I said. "Imagine that, right now, there's a knock on the door and Jesus himself walks into our room. Imagine he sits down in front of you all and says, 'Ok. Here I am. I've got all the time in the world. Ask me every single question you've got, and I promise I'll answer them all.' How long do you think it would take to get through all our questions?"

They all thought about it for a moment, and then one girl said, "Probably about ten thousand years".

And she was absolutely right.

Actually, the true answer is probably closer to *forever*, because the thing about an infinite God is that there are an infinite number of questions we could ask him.

And it's great to keep asking those questions. But, as I was trying to explain to this class, we need to keep in mind that every answer we find is going to open up even *more* questions: not because God is being tricky or secretive but because he's so awesome and wondrous and *huge*—and because truth always leads to *more truth*.

The class was quiet for a second, and then a girl piped up with something I've been thinking about ever since: "You know what, Mr Morphew? If Jesus came into the classroom, I don't think I'd want to ask him any questions. I think I'd just go up and give him a hug."

The more I think about it, the more I realise just how perfect that girl's response was.

When we suffer, it raises all kinds of questions about God, and it can be easy to think that if we could just wrap our *heads* around the answers to those questions, we'd feel a whole lot better.

But actually, I'm not so sure that's true—because, like I said way back at the beginning of this book, suffering isn't just a puzzle for our heads. It's a problem for our hearts.

And so when we suffer, what if what we need most isn't a perfect set of *reasons* for it?

What if all we really need to know is that we're not alone, that we're loved, and that we're going to be ok in the end?

Because in Jesus, that's exactly what we get.

He loved you enough to die for you. Whatever the reasons for our suffering, we can look to the cross and be sure that it's *not* because God doesn't love us.

And he was strong enough to overpower death itself. Whatever the reasons for our suffering, we can look to the empty tomb and be sure that it's *not* because God isn't powerful enough to help.

When Jesus comes back, maybe he'll sit us down and answer all our questions about our pain and our suffering, and why he let this or that horrible thing happen to us. Or maybe we'll just be so wrapped up in his love that all our complaints and our questions will just fall away.

When Jesus comes back, maybe we won't want to ask him that many questions after all.

Maybe we'll just want to go up and give him a hug.

$$\sim\!\!\sim\!\!\sim\!\!\sim\!\!\sim$$

I don't know why Jesus let Alegra die—but I know her story isn't over yet.

Because I know Alegra loved Jesus.

And I know that after death comes resurrection.

And so I know that, as they put their hope in Jesus, Alegra's family and friends can look forward to the day when they'll see her again, healthy and invincible and free.

In the meantime, she's perfectly safe with Jesus.

∧∧∧∧∧∧∧

And so here we are, at the end of the book.

And if you're looking for a specific answer for *why* God let a particular awful thing happen in your life or in the life of someone you love...

I'm really sorry, but I don't have it.

I don't know why God let it happen.

I don't even know if finding out *why* would help very much.

But here's what I do know.

I know Jesus loves you deeply. I know he's right there with you in your suffering, and that his heart breaks right along with yours.

I know Jesus cares so much about the mess the world is in that he came here and died to offer us a way back home to him.

I know his resurrection is his unbreakable promise that things won't always be this way.

I know the day is coming when sickness and suffering and pain and death and betrayal and racism and war and *all* of the world's brokenness will be nothing but old stories that his people will tell each other to remind ourselves of the hugeness of the love and power that Jesus showed us by coming to our rescue.

I know that, in Jesus, God has given us something way better than a thousand clever answers. He's given us himself.

And I'm convinced that's more than enough.

References

Timothy Keller's preaching was immensely helpful as I was writing this book—it helped me see the connection between God's Spirit hovering over the waters at Creation and Jesus calming the storm on Lake Galilee, and also helped me put words to the idea that God's ultimate answer to our questions about him is not an argument, but a person. My illustration about the two kids scrubbing toilets is also adapted from a similar story I heard Keller tell in one of his sermons.

This book also owes a debt of gratitude to Tim Mackie and Jon Collins, whose Bible Project podcast helped me better understand the connections between ancient mythology and the true story of the Bible.

The line in Chapter 9 of this book about how "the world will be even more beautiful for once having been so sad" is borrowed from *The Jesus Storybook Bible* by Sally Lloyd-Jones.

Thank yous

Thanks to Sue-Ellan, Marino, Emmanuela, and Strato, for letting me share some of Alegra's story in this book. May our great God continue to bless and strengthen you as you trust in him.

Thanks to Rachel Jones for being such an insightful and patient editor, to André Parker for his awesome design, to Emma Randall for the fantastic illustrations and cover artwork, and to the whole team at TGBC for getting behind this series and helping it to be the best it can be.

Huge thanks to Hannah Chalmers, Micah Ford, Corlette Graham, Ella and Fran Jewell, Hannah, Grace, and Georgie Moodie, and Sophia Tollitt, for reading early drafts of this book. Your insights and encouragement have been incredibly helpful.

Thanks to the staff, students and families of PLC Sydney. It is one of the great privileges of my life to share the good news of Jesus with you every week. In particular, thanks to my 2020 Year 5 classes—5B, 5E, 5O, and 5W—who heard these books first, and provided heaps of useful feedback.

Thanks to Mum and Dad for the countless hours you've poured into talking through my big questions about God over the past 30+ years.

Thanks to Katie and Waz, Phil and Meredith, and Kerryn and Andrew, for your constant love, support, wisdom, and encouragement.

Thanks to Hattie, for helping me see the love of God more clearly. May you grow up full of big questions, and may you keep turning back to our great king Jesus for the answers.

Thanks to Tom French for being a brilliant writing and podcasting buddy.

Thanks to Rowan McAuley for your friendship and partnership in the gospel, and for being so constantly enthusiastic and encouraging about these books, even though they keep dragging me away from the novels we're meant to be writing.

Last but not least, thanks to my church family at Abbotsford Presbyterian. In particular, a huge shout-out to the whole crew at YCentral—may this book help you to see even more clearly the abundant love God has for you in Jesus.

Keep asking big questions:

△ △△△ △△ △△ △

Big Questions is a series of fun and fast-paced books walking you through what the Bible says about some of the big questions of life, helping you to grow in confident and considered faith.

 thegoodbook.co.uk/big-questions
thegoodbook.com/big-questions
thegoodbook.com.au/big-questions

Also by Chris Morphew:

A devotional 100-day journey through Mark's fast-paced, action-packed story—bringing you face to face with Jesus: the one who changes everything.

thegoodbook.co.uk/best-news-ever
thegoodbook.com/best-news-ever
thegoodbook.com.au/best-news-ever

thegoodbook
COMPANY

BIBLICAL | RELEVANT | ACCESSIBLE

At The Good Book Company, we are dedicated to helping Christians and local churches grow. We believe that God's growth process always starts with hearing clearly what he has said to us through his timeless word—the Bible.

Ever since we opened our doors in 1991, we have been striving to produce Bible-based resources that bring glory to God. We have grown to become an international provider of user-friendly resources to the Christian community, with believers of all backgrounds and denominations using our books, Bible studies, devotionals, evangelistic resources, and DVD-based courses.

We want to equip ordinary Christians to live for Christ day by day, and churches to grow in their knowledge of God, their love for one another, and the effectiveness of their outreach.

Call us for a discussion of your needs or visit one of our local websites for more information on the resources and services we provide.

Your friends at The Good Book Company

thegoodbook.com | thegoodbook.co.uk
thegoodbook.com.au | thegoodbook.co.nz
thegoodbook.co.in